BUSINESS SUCCESS GUIDES

How to Negotiate a Bigger Raise

George M. Hartman

CASSELL

A CASSELL BOOK

First published in the UK 1995
by Cassell
Villiers House
41/47 Strand
London
WC2N 5JE

Copyright © 1991 by Barron's Educational Series, Inc.

Published by arrangement with Barron's Educational Series, Inc.,
Hauppauge, NY

All rights reserved. No part of this book may be reproduced or
transmitted in any form or by any means, electronic or mechanical,
including photocopying, recording or any information storage and
retrieval system, without prior permission in writing from the
copyright holder and Publisher.

Distributed in Australia
by Capricorn Link (Australia) Pty Ltd
2/13 Carrington Road
Castle Hill
NSW 2154

British Library Cataloguing in Publication Data
A catalogue record for this book is available from the British Library

ISBN 0-304-34458-3

Printed and bound in Great Britain by
Biddles Ltd, Guildford and King's Lynn

CONTENTS

INTRODUCTION:

*Getting
the Broad
Picture*

CHAPTER 1

NEGOTIATE THAT RAISE; DON'T WAIT FOR AN "AUTOMATIC" INCREASE

I believe that people most directly involved—whose lives and destiny are most directly affected—should always be parties to the negotiations in which their future is being decided.

—*Jeane Kirkpatrick*

So you've decided that it's time for a raise! But before taking action, you need a battle plan. Here are some things to consider:

- your worth, as a middle manager, to the company—specifically, why you deserve a bigger paycheck;
- the salary/fringe benefits limits you are willing to accept;
- the salary levels and policies prevailing in your company;
- your supervisor's probable reaction to your request;
- the strategies and tactics you will need to negotiate the raise you want.

Later chapters will deal with these topics in detail. The purpose of this Introduction is to encourage you to go after the sizable increase you deserve, to introduce you to negotiation techniques, to convince you that you can learn to negotiate effectively, and to help you assess the limitations on what you can reasonably expect.

PRINCIPLE 1

If a CEO's average raise is 30 percent per annum and a production worker's is 5 percent, certainly a manager's raise should be somewhere in between these extremes.

1. Measuring Your Worth

In her article "Caught in the Middle," Amanda Bennett reports, "When it comes to compensation, what makes middle managers see red? . . . What makes middle managers mad is unfairness." Ask managers to describe why they feel this way and, without hesitation they will usually point to the inequities of corporate salary structures — specifically, the difference between their own salaries and their bosses' or CEOs' compensation. They will gripe about not getting recognition for job performance where it counts — in their wallets.

"Corporate America is split by a gulf between top management and everybody else — in pay, in perks, in self-importance" — so states Alan Farnham in *Fortune* magazine. In the 1980s, the CEO's average compensation increased approximately 300 percent over the ten-year period, whereas the production worker gained only 50 percent. Says Farnham, "The Hay Group, drawing on ten years of survey data — hundreds of companies, thousands of employees — concluded in a 1988 study that the attitudes of middle managers and professionals toward the working place are becoming more like those of hourly workers, historically the most disaffected group." From another survey, "a growing 'perception gap' between what employees really want and what top management 'thinks' they want" was reported.

So where does the manager fit in? How does a company determine what a manager is worth? Who establishes what is the right salary for a particular quality of service? The subject of worth is covered in more detail in Chapters 3 and 4. Chapter 4 discusses the salary administration techniques used by the human resource departments of many companies. These techniques help in grading jobs and in evaluating performance and other relevant factors to establish salaries and salary-level ranges.

Unlike managers, CEOs and production workers can at least cope with inflation; their salaries and wages tend

5

to keep pace with cost-of-living increases. However, when it's their turn for raises, many managers find themselves at the mercy of their bosses. When a company is doing well, its managers may receive salary increases that are reasonably comparable, in terms of percentages, to those of production workers. But when times are bad, many companies limit raises, and the managers are frequently the last to be considered. CEOs will still get their base salaries; or, if asked to resign, they may float away beneath "golden parachutes." And production workers will probably get their raises right on schedule, especially if they are unionized.

A CEO's compensation may include a base salary, bonuses, and perks (for example, a company car). Long-term incentives, such as options to purchase company stock, may be added and extended over many years. A similar type of compensation arrangement might well be considered for managers.

So sharpen your wits—and, of course, your negotiating skills—and get ready to do battle by showing not only what you are worth today but also what a valuable asset you have been and will be to your company and, especially, to your supervisor.

2. An Overview of Negotiation Techniques

In Jack Chapman's book, *How to Make $1,000 a Minute: Negotiating Salaries and Raises,* Richard Germann asks, "Is it true that you can negotiate anything? The answer is, 'Of course you can!' But will it do you any good? This requires a longer answer." People who are facing negotiations can be divided into three categories: those who don't try negotiating because they feel uncomfortable, don't know how, or have made up their minds it won't work; those who negotiate without plan or purpose and therefore to no effect; and those who see negotiating as a valuable skill to develop and practice conscientiously.

The art of negotiation requires skills and knowledge that come from experience, not from formal education.

But regardless of your experience or lack of it, when applying negotiation techniques you should know when to use strategies and tactics—and how to tell them apart:

- *strategy* consists of the plans developed in preparation for a negotiation session;
- *tactics* are extemporaneous methods of reaching agreements.

Negotiation is successful when both parties profit from it. This mutual benefit should be your goal when you begin to negotiate for a pay increase. After all, you will probably be dealing with your supervisor on many other occasions if you both remain with the company.

The goal of the negotiation process is winning. Therefore, your strategy must include gaining insight into these factors: your performance and profit motivation, company needs, salary versus position, available options, and the company's financial condition. You should also consider ways to control the tempo of the negotiation without appearing to be in command.

Your negotiation skills should include the ability to communicate effectively, to observe and read people, and most important, to think on your feet. The quality of your communication is demonstrated by how well you present your case and how readily it is comprehended and accepted. On the other side of the coin, you must listen carefully to what is being said. Prior knowledge of your supervisor's personality, needs, and goals can help you to negotiate more effectively.

3. Yes, You Can Be an Effective Negotiator

What makes a negotiator effective? Whether you are negotiating for a salary increase or a contract, you should consider this question carefully. For a negotiator, the three most desirable qualities are aspiration, skill, and self-confidence. With these three (plus a dash of power, which will be discussed last), a negotiator should get the desired results.

7

Let's consider each of the three qualities separately.

Aspiration has a big influence on the outcome of a negotiation. The negotiator with a high level of aspiration has a strong desire to win. On the other hand, fear of failure is characteristic of a low aspiration level.

Skill includes knowledge of negotiation techniques—strategies and tactics—and good communication. (Skill techniques necessary to negotiate are described in Chapter 7.)

Self-confidence is usually acquired through maturation and experience. A negotiator must think well of him- or herself in order to project a favorable impression.

A moment's reflection reveals that these three important qualities are closely interrelated. If you have high *aspiration* to succeed, you will recognize the need for the negotiating *skills* that will enable you to prevail. In turn, by acquiring these techniques, you will greatly increase your level of *self-confidence*. And from all three will come a heady sense of *power*—a conviction that you can control events and people to achieve your purpose.

As an effective negotiator, you will also need other skills and qualities:

- *Ability to plan:* Perhaps the most productive time in the negotiation process is spent in planning, including the capability of showing your worth and being prepared with an activity log. (Worth and the activity log are covered in Chapters 3 and 5, respectively.)
- *Ability to think clearly under stress:* During the salary-review session, you will no doubt experience stress, so you must be able to think under pressure.
- *Good listening habits:* You should be capable of responding to questions with logical replies. This requires an ability to listen carefully and attentively.
- *Good verbal skills:* You must be able to express your requirements clearly and effectively in speech and in writing.
- *Ability to gain respect* from your supervisor and anyone else in the organization. This is an essential quality for

a manager and should be reflected in your role as a negotiator.

- *Empathy:* Sensitivity to the feelings of others will help you to establish and maintain good rapport with your supervisor.
- *Personal integrity:* You should represent yourself without exaggeration and without distortion of facts.

Finally, there are certain personality traits that are linked with exceptional managerial skills. To evaluate your own personality, ask yourself the following questions (excerpted from Christopher Hegarty and Philip Goldberg's book, *How to Manage Your Boss*):

- Are you a self-starter?
- Do you have good vibes about other people?
- Can you lead others?
- Can you take responsibility?
- Are you a good organizer?
- Are you a good worker?
- Can you make decisions?
- Can people trust what you say?
- Can you stick with a job?
- Are you in good health?

If you can answer yes to all of these questions, you probably deserve a big raise. Go for it—don't settle for an average amount or for an "automatic" increase that reflects just time on the job, rather than outstanding performance as a manager.

CHAPTER 2

RECOGNIZING LIMITATIONS:

*You versus
Your Supervisor*

We judge ourselves by what we feel capable of doing, while others judge us by what we have already done.

—Henry W. Longfellow

You've decided to ask for a raise, and you've gained some idea of negotiation techniques and the personal qualities needed to negotiate effectively. Now, since this isn't a case of the sky's the limit, you should consider the practical limitations on what you can reasonably expect to achieve. This chapter covers some topics associated with these limitations; identifying factors that determine compensation, examining your needs and wants, establishing an acceptable salary range, and analyzing your supervisor's position and personality.

PRINCIPLE 2

Know your adversary.

1. CEO Salaries

By any measurement, CEOs' worth seems to be somewhat independent of their performance. Several *Fortune* magazine studies over recent years have identified six factors that determine what CEOs and other top managers are paid.

Performance: A 10 percent improvement in performance can result in a raise of 25 to 30 percent.

Location: Working in New York City, where the cost of living is high, may mean 10 to 35 percent more in pay. Only Los Angeles comes close to New York in levels of compensation.

Business risk: A rise in business risk of 10 percent may result in a 5 percent increase in pay.

Size: The size of a company includes a combination of sales volume, assets, and shareholders' equity. A 10 percent increase in size may raise a CEO's salary by 2 percent.

Industry: CEOs of power utilities are paid the least, followed by CEOs of transportation and retailing concerns.

Tenure: As a rule, a CEO of long standing earns less than a new hiree. A CEO's salary may decrease by 6 percent for every 5 additional years with the same company.

Even though you're not yet a CEO, the preceding information may be helpful in that the same six factors may also influence a manager's salary.

In another survey of 225 CEOs done by *Chief Executive* magazine, two thirds of the respondents indicated a belief that pay has a direct correlation with performance and that long-term incentives should be emphasized.

2. Examining Your Needs and Wants Before a Salary Review

When you request a raise, your supervisor's initial response may be, "Why do you think you deserve an increase?" For this reason, prime prerequisites in advance of a salary-review meeting include adequate preparation and job performance above expected levels. When challenged, be specific in stating how you've exceeded expectations. Be ready to list your accomplishments, to explain their benefit to the company, and to describe what you see as your role in the firm, both for the present and in the future.

To start, perform a self-appraisal by answering the following questions:

- Are you doing just your job, or more than is expected of you?
- Do you fit into the company's long-range plans, and are you promotable?
- What are your salary goals—now, a year from now, and in the next decade?
- Are you keeping up with your professional education?
- What are your performance goals and objectives—now and for the future?
- What are your strengths and weaknesses? (Do your strengths outweigh your weaknesses?)
- Would you seek employment elsewhere if you are denied a raise that is satisfactory to you?
- What can you do to improve your value to your firm?

3. Establishing a Range for Your Increase

Having gained a rough idea of the raise you want, give yourself latitude to negotiate the exact amount. Be prepared with a salary range that you consider acceptable. Your top figure may be higher than the one that has been established by the company for your position (see Chapter 4). Even so, your salary requirements should be based on how important your work is to both your supervisor and the company, and the company's apparent willingness to pay for it.

If you are aware of the company's range, you may want to take the initiative and present your salary requirement first. However, if you are uncertain of the range, let your supervisor, not you, make the initial offer. But before making a counteroffer, question the range: When was it last increased, and when will it be updated? Don't be surprised if your supervisor is reluctant to give you answers. Expect to hear some objections, such as "Company budgets are limited," "Other employees in your category are not making as much as you are now," and "This offer is a lot more than you are currently earning." If this happens, try using closing techniques (see Chapter 7), but first determine the reason(s) that your request is meeting resistance.

4. Understanding Your Supervisor's Viewpoint

When negotiating raises, you and your supervisor are, frankly speaking, adversaries. You want the highest raise you can get. Your supervisor wants to retain a productive and loyal worker at the lowest cost. His or her overall goal is to increase the workload while minimizing the number of employees, and to have these employees follow orders with a minimum number of questions and little need for direction and training. In addition, your supervisor wants to make an impression on his or her own superiors—to demonstrate outstanding performance as a leader, while reducing the number of problems being brought to the attention of upper management. How much your supervisor may be willing to give in return for your assistance in achieving company goals may depend on how well you've "sold" your worth, what you are willing to accept, and what compromises you both are willing to make. How easily you reach an agreement may depend on your replies to questions and how well you keep the salary discussion open until your objective is met.

An important factor with a direct impact on the negotiations is personalities—yours and your supervisor's. You should know how to recognize a person's social style and be aware of the different ways people interact. This knowledge can be useful in winning the other party's respect and acquiring the capability to anticipate his or her remarks and actions. The following are four common personality types:

- *Ambitious* types are oriented more toward achieving results than toward dealing with people. They appear uncommunicative and stable, and act independently and competitively in relationships with others. Most people who fall within this category have pleasant, even charming, personalities. However, they tend to slight other people, mainly through failure to recognize good work.

- *Extroverts* appear to be communicative, warm, and approachable, but they are also competitive. They may seem to seek your friendship but actually may only want you to follow and support their ambitions. Your relationship with an extrovert may continue only until he or she reaches a self-serving goal.
- *Friendly* types are the most "people oriented" of the personality styles. They treat people as individuals rather than as a means of achieving results or influence. They look for—and usually get—supportive opinions. They are friendly and warm, but they avoid taking risks.
- *Introverts* are uncommunicative, levelheaded, and independent. They may show cooperativeness, but are cautious in displaying friendliness and are mainly concerned with getting things done without any personal involvement.

PLANNING YOUR STRATEGY

CHAPTER 3

WHAT IS YOUR WORTH?

I got a million dollars' worth of advice and a very small raise.

> —*Eddie Stanky of the Brooklyn Dodgers,*
> *after negotiating with Branch Rickey*

In this part of the book (Chapters 3 to 6) the focus is on prenegotiation strategy: assessing your worth in the current job market and to your company; examining job evaluation, salary administration, and performance appraisal as practiced by the company; taking certain specific steps to prepare for the salary-review meeting; and predicting the negotiation tactics that your supervisor may use and planning how to meet them.

Hints for researching salary information are provided in this chapter, and various types of alternatives to raises, better known as "options" and "perks," are described.

PRINCIPLE 3

Job relevancy is important, but personal achievement is better.

1. Your Worth on the Open Market

Before negotiating for a salary increase, it is important to learn what your skills and abilities as a manager are worth in the open market, as well as to your company. One of the best ways to obtain this information is by exchanging salary information with others in similar positions, within and outside the company. Sometimes these peers may not be willing to reveal their own salaries but may volunteer information about the salaries of others. Personnel recruitment agencies are also a good source for determining salary levels as equated to years of experience. Also, many trade periodicals run surveys of salaries. The Bureau of Labor Statistics and even want ads are other good sources of information.

A survey conducted by *Compensation and Benefits Review* among 35 personnel managers and 234 middle managers from the same industry resulted in different opinions about salary raises. Responses from the personnel managers indicated the use of criteria based on factors other than performance. Middle managers, however, preferred pay raises based on performance and were dissatisfied with salary inequities. As a result of the survey, it was concluded that a rewards system for middle managers should be more equitable and incentives given to improve and recognize performance. Another conclusion was that improved managerial performance may help to improve a company's position in relation to the competition.

Now let's look specifically at your market value. A little research on your part will be helpful as a beginning. Your local library may have one or more of the following publications available:

- *The Occupational Outlook Handbook,* published by the United States Government Printing Office, describes tomorrow's jobs and comments on each with respect to the type of work, location of employment, training requirements, qualifications, advancement, current and future opportunities, and earnings.
- *American Almanac of Jobs and Salaries.*
- *National Survey of Professional, Administrative, Technical, and Clerical Pay*, published by the Bureau of Labor Statistics.
- *The Encyclopedia of Associations,* issued by Gale Research, lists 18,000 professional organizations.

■ Trade journals or magazines. (A letter or phone call to a publication may produce pertinent information.)

See Chapter 4 for information regarding salary administration techniques and their effect on your salary and potential raises.

2. Your Worth to the Company as a Manager

A manager's worth may be considered in terms of performance, peer acceptance, company politics, presentation of self, ability to resolve administrative problems, and skill at handling the pressures of the job. Level of performance may be indicated by how well critical problems are analyzed and solved, whether the manager does more than the job requires, and whether he or she is cooperative, accepts criticism well, and displays motivation. Let's look into some relevant factors.

Accepting responsibility: Failure cannot always be blamed on someone else or attributed to bad luck. When resources and personnel are provided to perform certain functions for a company, a manager must accept responsibility for both good or bad happenings. Mistakes do occur, but a manager should be able to analyze the causes and know how to institute corrective action for present and future problems.

Motivation: A manager may have knowledge, abilities, and skills but lack the motivation to produce. A department with an unmotivated manager is likely to show minimal results.

Self-knowledge: A manager must know his or her strengths and weaknesses. It is important to avoid trying to be what one is not. At the same time a manager must be willing to investigate and apply methods for improving traits and skills that are important for effective performance on the job.

Self-acceptance and acceptance of others: Self-acceptance should not lead to complacency; rather, it means recognizing one's limitations in making improvements. In regard to others, a manager should be sensitive to the needs of fellow managers, subordinates, and superiors. A manager should know how to criticize constructively and should also be able to accept criticism without animosity.

3. The Question of Fringe Benefits

When negotiating a raise, a good time to discuss fringe benefits or perks is after you have obtained the highest possible salary increase. Then focus your negotiating skills on getting an improved package of fringe benefits. Remember that benefits come in two primary categories: *fixed* benefits that usually apply to all employees (e.g., health and pension plans), and *flexible* benefits that depend on job classification and may include tangibles such as a larger office with better furniture (and that prestigious carpeting!), free medical examinations, extra insurance coverage, relocation expenses, low-interest loans, flexible hours, a company car (for business and sometimes also for personal use), stock options (e.g., the right to purchase company stock at reduced market values), free legal and financial counseling, membership dues for professional associations and consumer price clubs, extra vacation or free time, a savings plan whereby the company may match part of the employee's savings, and a personal computer that may be kept at home or used while traveling.

Middle management is the level where you may expect to begin acquiring valuable perks (depending on the industry and your position within it). *Working Woman* magazine identifies six perks "that make your salary worth more":

- Interest-free loans, which may cover the purchase of a house.
- Bonuses for accepting positions at higher levels of the company.

- Spousal-assistance benefits for company transferees, whereby a company finds a spouse a job in the new location or provides retraining.
- Health-club membership, as a corporate member or under a company-paid sponsorship.
- Financial planning assistance.
- A "golden parachute" in the event of future layoff.

Other types of supplements or alternatives to salary increases may include:

- Commissions and bonuses, such as higher commissions on sales above a set quota, profit sharing, or performance bonuses.
- Cars and expense accounts. A company car can be worth thousands since the company pays for insurance and maintenance. Expense accounts are usual for sales personnel.
- Professional dues and reimbursement for expenses incurred for meetings.
- Time off for meetings or for training sessions.
- Additional vacation and personal days.
- Extra payment for time worked, including holiday premiums, overtime, and shift differentials.
- Payments for time not worked, such as holidays, jury duty, medical leave, sick leave, personal days, and vacation days.
- Various employee services, including a low-cost cafeteria, athletic team sponsorship, a company store, school-tuition reimbursement, and free work clothes.
- Increased financial benefits, such as company contributions toward insurance, stock-purchase plans, and pensions.

CHAPTER 4

SALARY ADMINISTRATION AND COMPENSATION

There is no success without hardship.

—*Socrates*

During your negotiation for a raise, your supervisor may frequently refer to "company policy about salaries." Since salary administration will certainly affect the outcome of the negotiation, this chapter deals with the topic in detail so that you can include this important element in your planning.

It is no surprise that organizations assign salaries according to the difficulty and importance of job categories. Compensation for these job-related factors usually falls into two categories: (1) equal pay for equal work, and (2) more pay for jobs requiring more responsibilities.

To assist companies in the determination of salaries, job-evaluation methods are established by salary administrators of human resources departments. These administrators, with the assistance of members of management, often compare jobs via various formal and systematic procedures to determine the relative positions of jobs to each other and to salary levels. The basis of any technique utilized is to consider each job in terms of its relative importance to the firm. Furthermore, any chosen method ranks jobs and compares factors involved in performance, such as skills, education, and experience, as well as responsibilities. This is followed by an appraisal system to rate employees and to assist management in salary reviews.

PRINCIPLE 4

Job evaluations and appraisals may measure managerial performance, but without adequate raises they are meaningless.

The objectives of a job-evaluation and performance-appraisal system include:

- Providing workable wage structures in a systematic way.
- Setting up rates for new or revised job classifications.
- Providing a means to compare wage and salary rates within departmental groupings.
- Providing a base against which individual performance can be measured.
- Providing incentives for employees to strive for higher-level positions.
- Providing data to assist management by listing requirements for training, transfers, and promotions.

The amount of a particular raise may be selected from within preestablished salary ranges and may depend greatly on future business plans (or projected revenues). A company may decide to improve its salary levels in order to acquire managers who are considered the "cream of the crop" in the labor market. The company may expect to obtain or retain better leadership by paying more than its competitors. On the other hand, the reality of corporate economics may force a company to pay employees the minimum and dilute their responsibilities. In this case, upward adjustment of wage levels may occur only in response to excessive labor turnover and absenteeism.

To help determine salaries, companies may refer to information on labor markets and review current economic conditions, recent union settlements, and future prospective revenues. A factor of lesser importance may be cost-of-living standards versus community location.

1. Job Standards and Salary Administration

For skilled workers the salary ranges and wage increases established will depend on the types of workers to be recruited, differentials between labor categories, and employee demands. The number of steps within a range and its bandwidth (i.e., low to high value) will depend on the period of time allowed for an employee to achieve proficiency in the skills required for the job.

Determining a manager's market value may be more difficult since job requirements may not be as well defined as those for lower-echelon positions. Professionals often have staff positions, and many in-line managers believe that they function like professionals. Since the work of a professional involves tasks few others can perform, evaluation (by the company) of a professional can be most difficult. Duties may be identified by employing generic job descriptions. Maturity curves, which show age (usually in terms of years since receiving the first degree) versus monthly salary, may be used in addition to job-evaluation or performance-appraisal methods to provide recognition to those with more years of excellence and proven loyalty. (See next page for a typical maturity curve.)

Salary levels often depend on salary surveys of an overall industry; here, the basis of compensation is the job market. Also, salaries of managers may be influenced by the relationship of their pay to that of their subordinates. Professional organizations can provide salary information obtained from surveys that may be categorized by age, years of experience since attainment of a degree, and rated job performance. In some cases private salary surveys, conducted by a company or a consulting firm, may be required to determine regional versus global salary differences.

As stated above, job evaluation (or standards) relates all job categories in a company to each other and provides

A Typical Maturity Curve

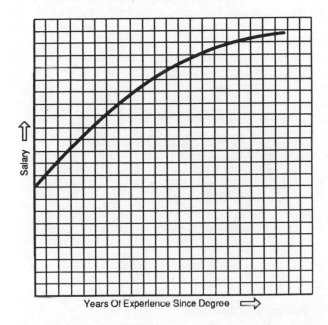

Years Of Experience Since Degree ⇨

wage scales. This rational but complex system of compensation requires administrators with good judgment skills. A job-evaluation system is concerned primarily with job categories and secondarily with the people who fill the positions in these categories.

Creating job standards may involve the following steps:

- Conducting a job study or analysis of required work output.
- Deciding on the criteria that make one job more valuable than another to management.
- Choosing a job-evaluation system that correlates jobs.
- Using a committee (drawn from management) to review and approve a program and to price each job level.

A survey reported in a later section reveals that a common method of salary structuring is based on a point-factor system. Each occupation is rated according to established factors. Each factor is weighted and assigned a number of points. Then the points are totaled to determine a point score for each job category. Once jobs are rated, pay scales are assigned. Salary levels within each category are correlated to a formula that links points and pay levels.

Typically, job factors may include:

1. Knowledge and skills (including experience and internal and external relationships and dexterity)   60–280 points
2. Mental demands (or physical effort)   8–140
3. Accountability (responsibilities: in-line supervisory or staff advisory)   11–160
4. Working conditions (hazards, location, etc.)   0–20

As would be expected, the higher the point total, the more a job is worth.

2. Performance Appraisals

Perhaps your company employs a performance-rating system that evaluates an employee's performance and can influence the size of a raise. The system may include a performance appraisal that is initiated by the supervisor, reviewed by both the employee and the supervisor, emended to resolve disagreements, and signed by both parties before its submittal to the human resources department. A performance appraisal, which is exclusive of any discussion of raises, precedes a merit review, the latter depending on results of the appraisal. The appraisal may be designed to highlight your assets and liabilities. Perhaps you may gain time to improve your deficiencies and to demonstrate superior performance; then, at the salary-review meeting, the improvements may influence the size of the raise you can negotiate.

Both the performance appraisal and the merit review should be conducted on a regular basis. If they fall behind schedule, this is cause for concern; any delinquency can affect your salary adversely since all future increases are based on percentages of your current salary. With the effects compounded over a number of years, continual late reviews will be reflected in a salary lower than you deserve.

3. Results of a Survey of Managers' Compensation

In a recent survey conducted by the author, directors and managers of human resources departments were asked for their opinions, as salary administrators, on the importance of six factors in determining raises for managers of their organizations. The personnel queried included representatives from both large and small firms. As might be anticipated, they unanimously ranked performance on the job as the top factor. The others—seniority/tenure, outside market value, size of firm, location of firm, and profitability of firm—received inconsistent rankings. The administrators were also asked to name any other factor(s) that they thought should be considered. The gamut ran from the individual (skill) needs of a firm—education and specialty—to compensating for inequities within salary levels. In reply to a question regarding the most influential factor in granting a manager a higher than average raise, the answer was again unanimous: outstanding performance!

Although many companies in the survey used the popular Hay (see box on page 33) and maturity curve methods in determining salary structure, most preferred to either adapt these methods to "custom-made" point-factor systems or to establish their own systems for market comparisons and employee appraisals. However, whatever systems were employed, the companies considered them proprietary and would not reveal details.

Although few organizations recognize age or seniority as contributors to experience, most pay ranges involve some movement based on seniority. Higher level jobs seem to be filled with higher seniority people. Maturity curves usually show that salaries level off after approximately 25 years.

In regard to the raises that are awarded within their firms, the administrators in the survey provided the following information:

- A normal raise varies from 4 to 8 percent, the average being close to 6 percent.
- An above-normal raise ranges from 8 to 12 percent, with raises that accompany promotions running from 10 to 15 percent.
- A large raise for a manager averages 12 percent; the low end is at 8 percent, and the high may reach 20 percent in exceptional cases. Most administrators indicated that a raise above 10 percent is considered unusual.

The Hay method of establishing salary structures compares about fifteen to twenty "key jobs" to factors that are common to all positions within a company. These factors typically include mental skill and physical requirements; responsibility; and working conditions.

The key jobs are ranked by order of importance of each factor. The process is repeated weekly for three weeks. The salaries of the key jobs are then rated by splitting the current salaries by the ranked factors. The result is dollar ranking versus the factors for each key job. For the other jobs within the company, the factor system is applied and the wages or salaries to be paid are added according to the dollar-ranked factors.

This method provides an evaluated rate for each salaried position. However, it is not useful for determining salary ranges at each job level.

CHAPTER 5

PREPARING FOR SALARY-REVIEW MEETINGS

Firmness in support of fundamentals, with flexibility in tactics and methods, is the key to any hope of progress in negotiation.

—*Dwight D. Eisenhower*

Your preparation for any salary-review meeting should include the following four items:

- Establishing and maintaining a personal activity log.
- Making yourself aware of relevant salary statistics.
- Improving your profitability to the firm, and demonstrating your worth.
- Establishing the salary and options that will be acceptable to you.

Let's consider each of these items separately.

PRINCIPLE 5

Plan your moves; then move your plans.

1. Establish and Maintain a Personal Activity Log

It is recommended that you keep an up-to-date job journal, recording significant accomplishments from the first day of your employment with the firm. Record your achievements and ideas for making progress, referring specifically to material in your field. Be sure to include a record of your past raises, with dates and percentages; a graphical presentation may be advantageous. Study your business associates (your supervisor, subordinates, subcontractors, customers), and record anything that may be significant as an indication of their skills versus yours.

Any time you receive a commendation, make sure it is in writing and placed with your activity log. If the human resources department maintains a personnel docket system, request access to it periodically. Retain a file of ways in which you have improved your performance over the current period to the benefit of the firm, including courses taken to improve your skills, accomplishments beyond the routine work tasks, awards received within and outside the company, articles written for trade publications, and professional projects in which you were involved.

In addition, keep your resume current. Your resume states your qualifications, which may sometimes be challenged during a negotiation.

2. Be Aware of Relevant Salary Statistics

As far as possible, familiarize yourself with your company's salary administration policies (see Chapter 4), including the creation of wage levels, frequency of raises, and methods of rating jobs. Research the field of your expertise to determine what other firms are paying managers with similar skills (see Chapter 3). Study survey reports. Place yourself within various salary structures, and determine your worth to the firm and to the outside market.

Researching the local library for periodicals with current information from salary surveys can be helpful. Here are examples from two types of trade magazines:

1. *Personnel Psychology* reports on personnel managers' salary-raise decisions for 104 hypothetical employees categorized by performance level, consistency of performance, tenure, current salary, and outside market value. Substantial differences noted in the ranking and the weighting of the various categories by the individual managers accounted for variances in the raise decisions.

2. Sumer and Sudhir Aggarwal report in *Personnel Journal* that firms need reward systems to assure loyalty, increase productivity, and facilitate the recruiting of new employees. Studies indicated that many firms have reward programs for managers based on the corporation's annual profit and that firms recognize the need to emphasize long-term benefits. An award system of longer than a year's duration is also described as a means to encourage improved performance and retain managers for longer periods.

3. Improve Your Profitability to the Firm, and Be Ready to Document It

In Dennis Kravetz's book *Getting Noticed,* the author points out, "A key component of long-term success is to keep aspiring to greater and greater things. When highly successful people accomplish one set of goals, they start working toward a new set immediately. People tend to work at their best when they are learning, developing, and feeling challenged on the job. When the job becomes routine, motivation wanes."

You demonstrate to your company how necessary and how profitable you are when you make things happen. The actual work may be done by your subordinates, but your administrative abilities—your direction and control—lead to accomplishment and results. Become an expert in your area of responsibility, so that others will seek you out and recognize you as a reliable source of information. Improve your knowledge of company operations and policies, both within and outside your department. Be recognized as a high achiever by accepting more than your share of work and delivering good results. If given the opportunity or responsibility, hire top-notch subordinates who will earn you respect and credibility as a leader. Be friendly to all personnel on all levels of the company; recognize people as individuals but avoid office politics, which can backfire very badly. You can end up rubbing the right people the wrong way.

In his book *Playing to Win*, Fran Tarkenton approaches the value of an employee to a company in another way. "When people ask me how to get a 'winning attitude,' I tell them there is no such thing as a winning attitude. There is only a *winning performance*." This concept usually starts at the top of an organization and trickles down through the various branches. Unless this description fits the organization in which you are employed, perhaps you had better plan on prospecting for a new job elsewhere. Your superiors may be sitting on you, figuratively speaking, and denying you the opportunity to be a self-motivator and to demonstrate outstanding performance.

But let's explore Tarkenton's method. He developed a procedure, using the acronym PRICE, which he claims may provide steps for creating a winning performance:

P = Pinpoint *any measurable performance of yours that needs to be changed.*

R = Record *the performance on a chart for everyone to see.*

I = Identify *the results of the performance: how much money or time is lost as a result of inattention or a job poorly done; then* intervene *to modify the performance.*

C = Change the consequences *of that behavior; give reinforcement and performance feedback in the form of praise and recognition.*

E = Evaluate *the changes in job performance; continue to review yourself or your employees and modify the consequences based on the direction of progress.*

How you achieved performance goals since your last raise and what you plan to achieve after you receive your next increase should be considered. Always use specific figures to support any claims of increased productivity, new skills acquired, labor-hours saved, and long-term benefits that you have initiated, such as improved employee morale and new product developments.

How does your compensation differ from the salaries of your subordinates? There should be an ample difference to adequately differentiate management status from lower levels. This difference serves to motivate those reporting to you to set their goals on replacing you as you move up the ladder in the organization. Of course, you may seek increased compensation for subordinates who demonstrate superior performance. In that case the salary gap may shrink and provide you with another reason to request a larger paycheck.

Superior performance certainly merits acknowledgment, by your supervisor and by management, that you are an outstanding manager and an excellent team leader, whose efforts help make the firm profitable.

4. Establish Acceptable Salary and Option Limits

How do you establish what you consider an uppermost acceptable salary limitation? In Chapter 3, the subject of job worth was emphasized as a major concern for the raise seeker. Before establishing any limit, you should examine the slope of a maturity curve showing pay distribution to see where you best fit in respect to your position and where you think you should fit relative to your performance. Do you think you are being compensated fairly, on the basis of the pay distribution curve?

In your review, you may discover inequities in your salary as compared with the compensation of fellow managers on the same level. Alternatively, the outside market may be competing for experienced individuals like you. These disclosures may assist you in the negotiation. As stated previously, however, the best weapon is a reasonable salary range and a list of perks (with dollar equivalents) to supplement the salary that you plan to demand.

CHAPTER 6

PREDICTING YOUR SUPERVISOR'S MOVES

*One man's word is no man's word; we
should quietly hear both sides.*

—*Goethe*

et's come back now to your superior, that adversary
figure in the negotiation whose personality and motives
were briefly considered in Chapter 2. Here we'll attempt a fuller analysis of what makes this important individual tick, so to speak, and we'll outline a one-to-one
strategy for success in your salary negotiation.

Now, either you are aware of your supervisor's traits
or you must get to know him or her better. In that respect, you should not enter the raise negotiation "cold"!
Watch out for power-game tactics that your supervisor
may play, and learn how to play along. Be prepared to
accept some criticism, even if it appears abusive, whims-
ical, or insensitive. Anticipate your supervisor's critical
questions ("What have you accomplished lately"?) and
statements ("You've only been here for a short time";
"You're at the top of the range now"; "You may be doing
excellent work now, but once I give you a raise you'll
probably relax"). Some of these arguments may sound
familiar to you.

PRINCIPLE 6

*You probably won't get everything you ask for, but
you can surely try!*

1. Getting to Know Your Boss

In Christopher Hegarty and Philip Goldberg's book *How to Manage Your Boss*, one of the authors states, " 'My boss doesn't understand me' is a complaint I hear quite frequently. Sometimes it's a valid statement, because many bosses do not understand, or even attempt to understand, their subordinates. However, the best and quickest way to get your boss to understand you is first to understand your boss."

Many business pressures may be hanging over a boss's head. Your supervisor may have been informed of cost-reduction requirements, a pressure builder that must be passed down the line. He or she may be concerned about applying strategies during the salary-review session that, if misunderstood, could backfire. It is essential to recognize that your supervisor is only human and, as such, is subject to the same frailties as you. As Hegarty and Goldberg point out, "Much of your relationship with your boss is determined by the way you perceive him. Change your perception and, in effect, you change your boss." In short, understand the responsibilities and pressures that he or she may be up against, and try a sympathetic approach. Your supervisor needs to be needed, and the reverse, it is hoped, is also true: you too are needed.

What about your supervisor's background? Have you seen his or her resume, or talked about education, business experience, sports, marital status? Is your supervisor active in professional, or civic organizations? Find out what your common interests are, and record them in your activity log book (see Chapter 5).

2. Using Positive Approaches

Many bosses feel that negotiating with an employee should turn out to be a win/lose situation. Your supervisor may also have been trained in negotiation techniques, particularly, in methods to get you to agree to what he or she wants you to think is reasonable. Let's look at some positive approaches that you can plan to use in a variety of situations:

- Keep your voice calm and well modulated. It's possible your supervisor may be watching whether you seem confident or nervous and may react accordingly. Watch your tone (and volume) of voice.
- Avoid confrontation. Preserve comradery by sticking to a "win/win" philosophy.
- Keep the discussion within your current and future period of employment; avoid being held responsible for mistakes the company made in the past.
- When questioned about future performance, ask your supervisor to apprise you of the company's or the department's future plans. Then both of you should discuss how well you fit into these plans.
- Keep the discussion lively and relevant; a dull or wandering session can end disastrously without much accomplished. Stick to the subject of your salary needs; don't be sidetracked.
- When asked a question, think before you respond; never fear a moment of silence.

3. Playing Along with "Power" Tactics

Be prepared, when reacting to your supervisor, to avoid open resentment or hostility. Let him or her talk! Perhaps your supervisor needs a sympathetic ear or a chance to blow off steam as a result of mounting pressures. Examine the situation for positive movements that may lead you into a "yes, but . . ." routine, in which you basically agree but do not totally acquiesce. If you like what you hear, give an affirmative response, but don't overdo it; few bosses appreciate yes-men or apple polishers.

Some supervisors with weak personalities may apply power tactics in an attempt to conceal insecurities. These people are not as powerful as they pretend they are, but you must play along with them. Never "bad-mouth" your supervisor!

By remaining firm and cool, you show flexibility and poise. You should seriously consider transferring to another department or even leaving the firm, however, if your supervisor stubbornly avoids responding to a request, whether it concerns salary or a promotion. Recognize delaying tactics; if requested to wait for a reasonable period, agree only when promised you will have a definite answer at the end of the waiting time. Always recognize that your supervisor should also expect a promotion or a raise in the immediate future, and be ready to help him or her get that advancement. As he or she moves up the corporate ladder, you will find an empty rung above you.

Dr. Warschaw, in her book *Winning by Negotiation*, identifies "The Power Game—and How to Play It with Each Stylist." Brief descriptions of the various stylists are provided below to assist you in classifying your supervisor. By recognizing the various types, you should have a better understanding of how to cope with each.

"Jungle fighters" love power and can be savage and merciless in pursuing their objectives, but can be handled. Avoid being intimidated, and don't let them think you fear them.

"Dictators" must be in control and will treat you as a follower. Avoid being used; but if you cooperate with and stick by them, you can provide valuable support to their egos.

"Silhouettes" are secretive about themselves and their motivations. Thus you may be required to draw upon outside sources for information about them. They may provide opinions but approach things quietly. Don't be afraid of silence, but answer questions directly and fully to hold their attention.

"Big mammas and daddies" control with love and approval and avoid power confrontations. Watch out lest you be treated like a child, for they may want to manipulate you into their way of thinking.

"Soothers" project a message that they need your

help, but they don't like to listen to your side of the story. They will deviate from the subject, so you must guide them back on track.

4. Anticipating What Your Supervisor May be Willing to Give

As described in Chapter 4, salary administration in a company consists of a formal program that provides management not only with job-evaluation methods but also with data on employee performance and salary statistics. Such a salary administration program defines acceptable performance measurements and attempts to recognize that better performers are entitled to higher pay. Salaries are distributed within certain ranges. The company's policy may include both automatic raises, which are given in steps, and merit raises, which are generally initiated by supervisors. Progression through ranges can be automatic, meritorious, or a combination of both, depending on the employee's skill and experience. Merit raises are based on the idea that wage increases should be earned through increased proficiency or quality of performance and viewed as incentives for future performance. Many managers, however, perceive all raises as identical and regard money in general as an incentive for future performance rather than as a reward for past achievement.

Pay raises within each salary range may be considered to hinge on the individual employee's performance, pay history, current position within the range, experience, time elapsed since the last raise, the amount of that raise, the salaries of others holding similar positions, labor-market considerations, and, most important, the company's financial condition.

So what can you expect from your supervisor? Will cost-of-living and any related salary adjustments be ignored? Will your supervisor blindly follow salary administration techniques or guidelines? Let's face it—your supervisor will prefer to offer you a salary in accordance with the going rate in a competitive market rather than meet what you feel you need for survival in inflationary times.

Okay, boss—you've reached the end of your rope, and you've run out of excuses for not providing a better raise. Let's go one step further! How about a promotion and the increase that accompanies it? A promotion certainly would open up a new rate range, as well as provide recognition for outstanding performance. But what about that "no opening for a promotion" response? If you can't get a satisfactory reply, you might plan to ask your supervisor to move you to another area or another department of the company that may provide an opportunity for advancement. But be cautious; avoid a threat to leave the company. An ultimatum may land you in the unemployment office. Regardless, your strategy should include a refusal to take a negative response as a final answer!

USING
WINNING
TECHNIQUES

CHAPTER 7

NEGOTIATION STRATEGIES AND TACTICS

Let us never negotiate out of fear. But let us never fear to negotiate.

—*John F. Kennedy*
Inaugural address,
January 20, 1961

The planning stage is over, and the big day is drawing near. It's time to consider the tactics that will result in a successful negotiation.

Because preparation is so important, however, let's first review and summarize some important prenegotiation strategies and tactics.

PRINCIPLE 7

To be considered successful, a salary negotiation should leave both parties feeling as though they have won something: you, a satisfactory raise; your supervisor, a contented, productive manager.

1. Preparation—the Key to Obtaining a Raise

Start with Yourself. To get the raise you're seeking, you must first establish plans and objectives to improve the areas of your performance that have a direct bearing on company efficiency, revenues, and profit. A solid record of outstanding work may be all that's required, as well as proof of an improving quality of performance. You should document your accomplishments, making sure that your supervisor acknowledges them, before attempting to negotiate a raise. Make sure that you have studied salary standards and have kept an activity log of your performance (see Chapter 5). As stated previously, establish your salary range—your target raise and your "bottom-line" raise; the latter will prevent you from accepting a less-than-satisfactory raise in the heat of the moment. Consider the most difficult issues that are likely to arise, and prepare alternatives or supplements to salary requirements (i.e., fringe benefits; see Chapter 3). Try predicting what objections your supervisor will raise and how you can overcome them.

Assess Your Supervisor and His or Her Position. If possible, be aware of some personal details about your supervisor: marital status, spouse's name, ages of children, hobbies, and any job-related interests that parallel yours, for example. Perhaps you can also find out something about his or her track record in awarding raises and promotions. To obtain this information, you may want to invite your supervisor to lunch or get together for an informal chat during or after working hours.

Most people are predictable. If a person does something once, he or she is likely to do it again. What can other people tell you about strategies your supervisor has used in the past? Is there anything on record that can give you clues?

Consider the decision-making hierarchy of your firm. With whom does your supervisor consult on salary administration matters? If he or she isn't authorized to get you a raise, who is?

Review your prior pay increases for frequency and rate. Seek out information about the frequency of increases given to your peers, how the raises compare to yours, the company's financial condition, and your department's current and future budgets.

Be Ready to Respond Effectively to Conflict. Conflict is a part of life. To get the raise you want, you may have to endure conflict, and you should be prepared for it. During the meeting you may say things your supervisor may not like or doesn't want to hear; therefore, you must expect negative reactions. Negotiating is by nature a stressful task, and the stress increases as the level of difficulty rises.

During a salary negotiation, belligerence and argumentativeness gain you nothing. Questions are much less threatening than statements. Whenever possible, phrase your statements in the form of questions. By remaining calm and courteous, you are more likely to achieve a successful outcome.

Improve Your Listening Skills. Practice active listening. During the negotiation you shouldn't stop listening to plan what you'll say next, or drift away because you think you know what your supervisor will say. Instead, plan to jot down notes. Probably your supervisor, even if sympathetic to your case, has some points to make. Patiently listen—and don't interrupt! If you don't understand what's being said, say so—and ask specific questions.

Ensure Physical Comfort and an Appropriate Setting. Here are some points to consider:

- Come to the meeting well rested and physically comfortable. Have adequate sleep the night before; eat sensibly, not gluttonously, before the meeting; and wear clothes and shoes that fit properly.
- Refrain from smoking, even if your supervisor smokes.
- If you have a choice, sit alongside your supervisor at his or her desk or at the conference table. (Sitting in front of your supervisor's desk or at the opposite side of the table creates the appearance of separation by rank.)
- Request that the meeting take place where there won't be any interruptions by other employees or by telephone calls. You will need the supervisor's undivided attention during the negotiation.

2. The Structure of the Negotiation

Most salary negotiations involve an offer-and-counteroffer sequence. Expect your supervisor to present an opening offer that is based on company salary administrative policies. Chances are the offer will be lower than what you consider acceptable. Therefore, you must be prepared to present the reasons you think you deserve a bigger raise. This counteroffer should be based on established objectives, such as an estimate of a reasonable range of salary increases and fringe benefits of comparable monetary value. (Chapter 5 contains advice on preparing for the salary-review meeting.)

Although your initial position will probably be higher than your supervisor's, it should not be so high that it precludes reaching agreement on a salary acceptable to you. You should be prepared, however, to accept an offer that is less than the high side of your objective, such as a percentage of increase that falls within your established range of acceptance (see Chapter 4).

Bear in mind that your supervisor may be bound by company policy to accept only a counteroffer that falls within his or her authority, even if a higher offer can be reasonably supported. If the company-authorized rate is below the lower end of your range, you will have to start applying your bargaining skills. You must be prepared to show, perhaps by citing your own extraordinary performance or comparable higher salaries for the same job, why the numbers must be bumped up.

3. Examples of Negotiation Strategies and Tactics

Salary negotiation involves varied techniques that are applied to enable the sessions to proceed amicably, without friction, so that an agreement satisfactory to both sides is readily reached. Experienced negotiators use a variety of means to accomplish their objectives. Knowing when to use a particular strategy requires a sense of timing. Negotiation techniques include both planned strategies and spontaneous or extemporaneous tactics.

Regardless of what transpires during the meeting, an atmosphere of mutual respect between the parties should be maintained at all times, especially if you and your supervisor work in a close relationship and expect to continue to do so over a long period.

Here are four commonly used strategies:

Combinations: To start, you may introduce simultaneously several positive factors in regard to your performance. In this way your supervisor may be forced to consider the broad picture. All points raised should be viewed as equally important. If your supervisor minimizes any of them at the time they are raised, you may wish to repeat some of them later.

Coverage: Some supervisors choose to avoid discussing details. They hope to conduct the meeting with as little time and effort as possible. However, you have a right to slow down the pace to provide adequate time for presenting each meritorious factor separately. After all, you expended considerable effort in preparing for the meeting, and you don't want this to go for nought. Your reasons for getting the raise must be properly addressed. Some supervisors obviously prefer a broad coverage, because if each factor is discussed separately, the rationale for minimizing a raise may be refuted.

Statistics: Each party should be certain that any figures and statistics that are presented are valid. Here again, preparation pays off. For example, if one party argues that certain statistical trends are representative of the future for the occupation in question, the other party should be prepared to reply.

One Step at a Time: Using this effective strategy, you convincingly present one point after another until your objective is reached. (Essentially, this is the antithesis of

coverage.) Each meritorious factor is addressed separately to emphasize your assets and value.

The four tactics described below are helpful in reaching an agreement:

Patience: This tactic involves delaying, suspending, or postponing an answer at the moment to give one party a chance to think over the other's proposition. However, the other side also has the same opportunity and may change his or her offer after further consideration. Any counteroffer should be withheld until it is felt that the other party will seriously reconsider the original proposition. This tactic is often useful when a supervisor responds to your demands with a statement such as "You've got to be kidding!"

Timing: The ideal time for initiating discussions about a raise may be when your supervisor comes into your office for a chat. However, you should keep this exchange informal; use it to set up a formal meeting at a later date that allows you adequate time for preparation.

Surprise: This requires a sudden shift in position. For example, you may request that your supervisor call in an immediate superior when an obstacle to reaching a salary agreement creates an impasse. Once the superior is included in the session, major factors should be reiterated and emphasized in the hope that the new negotiator is more reasonable and that a satisfactory agreement can be reached. However, this tactic is recommended only as a last resort, since it may offend your supervisor.

Diversion: This tactic calls for one party to exaggerate the information under discussion. Because this can be construed as a bluff, you should be cautious and avoid unfounded claims. Your supervisor is using the diversion tactic when he or she makes questionable promises about future raises in the hope that you will withdraw or reduce your present demands.

4. Closing Techniques

What do you do when you've tried applying salary-negotiation techniques but have failed to reach even a satisfactory compromise? How about trying closing techniques? Many sales personnel have certainly found them to be effective.

Some people possess proficiency in applying both negotiating and closing techniques. If you are among these lucky ones, you are blessed with powerful tools, but you must use them cautiously. You must be tactful to avoid upsetting your supervisor and to prevent him or her from becoming disenchanted with a loyal and productive manager. In particular, you need to avoid the possibility of being discharged.

Closing techniques are usually associated with sales but may be considered to be related to negotiating techniques in that both result in either "acceptance" or "rejection." In closing, however, rejection, which may mean that you have not been convincing enough to support your claim, is final; whereas, in negotiating, rejection may occur until agreement or a compromise is reached. Regardless of the techniques employed, your supervisor is likely to agree to a particular raise only when convinced that it is both reasonable and justifiable.

To clarify the primary *difference,* we may define *closing* as a technique employed by a seller (or, in our case, the seeker of a raise), whereas *negotiating* is used jointly by both a seller (you) and a buyer (in our case, your supervisor). Commonality between the two is most prevalent when sessions are deadlocked. In such cases the negotiation tactics ordinarily employed may very well be supplemented by closing techniques.

Closing, like negotiating, is an art requiring knowledge and skill, and is developed primarily through experience. It takes skill to read "ready-to-buy" signs and to overcome objections, as well as dexterity in applying negotiating techniques. Also, as a seeker your mental attitude should always be positive; you should be persistent but remain calm, alert, and ready for any element of surprise. To a certain degree, the closing technique requires acting ability—when it is time to be cordial, you perform accordingly; when it is time to be firm and dynamic, you rise dramatically to the occasion. You must know when to apply the appropriate tactic. You must sense when to talk (to ask questions) and when to shut your mouth (especially when you've reached the end of the line—your preplanned limitations). Your approach must suggest self-confidence; conceal any fear of failure.

If your supervisor seems unimpressed by your presentation, you should not get discouraged but should think in terms of "I failed to make him or her understand." Dust yourself off and *try again*! A common tactic is to use a positive "Yes, but . . ." approach. This leads the other party to think mistakenly that agreement has been reached and to relax his or her guard, offering you the opportunity to advance new arguments or emphasize old ones. Another tactic is to ask "Why?" in response to any item of disagreement. But make sure you keep quiet and listen to the answer!

Remember that the principle in handling objections is never to argue back. Simply reiterate: go over the same tracks, but use new arguments and clearer explanations. The temptation to "echo back" in a hostile way is always present and becomes greater as the negotiation drags on. You may win a particular argument; but in so doing, you may also antagonize your supervisor so that an agreement is less likely to be achieved.

5. Compromise—the Key to Reaching Agreement

In most cases, agreements result from compromises. The negotiation process requires both parties to aim toward achieving a settlement, and a compromise may be the only means of reaching agreement. In approaching a compromise, each party should attempt to summarize the other's position, pointing out specific areas of difference and presenting facts or opinions that support each position.

Some Aspects of Compromise. Commonly, each side establishes its "last" position before being willing to compromise. In the raise negotiation, two possible bases of agreement should be considered: a total raise now or progressive increases.

Two types of compromise are possible:

- Both sides feel a degree of satisfaction: an agreement has been reached for an acceptable "best" raise.
- One side is satisfied but not the other: because one party is stronger, an unbalanced compromise has been reached.

Tactical Mistakes to Avoid in Reaching an Agreement. To negotiate successfully, you should avoid the following mistakes:

Unreasonable opening demands: By aiming high, you give yourself room to negotiate. On the other hand, your opening demands should not be so unrealistic that your supervisor either postpones meeting with you or refuses to listen to what you have to say.

Free concessions: Never make a concession without getting one in return. Unconditioned concessions frequently turn into "freebies" for which your supervisor generally will not reciprocate.

Rapid negotiations: Rapid settlements are frequently extreme "win/lose" deals. The less prepared and the less skilled negotiator is often victimized by his or her opponent. Put yourself in command; slow things down.

Settling too quickly: Agreeing too quickly incurs a greater chance of not reaching or even nearing your objective. Be ready to "sleep on it," particularly if you have any doubts about accepting the raise offered. Resist any pressure for acceptance. Good deals are almost never bargained quickly.

Negotiating when surprised: Don't bargain unless you're fully prepared! If something unforeseen comes up, take a break. Ask your supervisor for time to review the proposition.

Fear of Silence: If you keep your mouth shut and show that you're listening, your supervisor may reciprocate. After you have asked a question or if you're in the process of thinking, keep quiet. Don't be embarrassed about long silences.

Getting angry: Keeping cool is a great advantage. Never lose your temper (at least, not obviously). Remember: You will probably continue to work with your supervisor after this review session. Also, emotion hampers the ability to think clearly. If you respond negatively to your supervisor, you may forget your prepared strategy and hence lose the "game"!

Failure to Get the Agreement in Writing: It is not enough just to reach an agreement; you need to get a written record. A handshake is fine, but ask your supervisor to put the agreed-to rate and perks in writing to avoid a lapse of memory. But be tactful in requesting the written agreement.

Negotiating when fatigued: Tired negotiators often make foolish errors and may be easily influenced by their opponents. For this reason be sure to get enough sleep the night before the meeting. Also, avoid drinking or smoking immediately before and while negotiating.

Letting your guard down: A few moments of carelessness can destroy the results of a hitherto-successful session. Your supervisor may have been waiting for his or her chance to take advantage of you. Don't relax until agreement has been reached.

Unduly prolonging the negotiation: In negotiating, as in playing poker, there's a time to hold and a time to fold. If you push too far, your irritated supervisor may react by calling off the meeting or even taking a more drastic step, such as getting rid of you.

Important Items to Remember about Negotiating: Here are some guidelines to keep in mind:

Failure to agree may be attributed to:

- Failure to provide adequate supporting arguments.
- A poor mental attitude.
- Offending your supervisor.

To avoid these causes of failure you must:

- Prepare thoroughly for the session.
- Listen carefully to what your supervisor has to say.
- Answer objections adequately (in detail, but just enough to hold your supervisor's attention and interest).
- If possible, turn objections around so that they become reasons to accept your arguments. For example, if your supervisor points out that you have been on the job only six months, you might respond that, far from seeing your work as routine, you still retain your original enthusiasm and high motivation.
- Avoid cockiness, sarcasm, and overt hostility.
- Dress neatly and appropriately.
- Maintain a positive attitude toward what is being said: listen attentively, and be alert and responsive.
- Present strong and convincing arguments.
- Display interest and enthusiasm.
- Be strong but *not* overpowering.

CHAPTER 8

YOU AS A NEGOTIATOR

You win by trying, not by standing around!

—*Fran Tarkenton*

Now it's time to take a look at you, especially in the role of negotiator. What kind of appearance do you present to your supervisor? What kind of signals do you project by your body language? Are you alert to the signals being conveyed to you? To complete this personal appraisal, consider your own behavior during the negotiation session, including self-evaluation of how you did.

PRINCIPLE 8

Stop: look at and listen to yourself, and visualize how others see you.

1. Your Appearance Counts

When you look into a mirror, you get a certain impression about yourself. To obtain the raise you deserve, you want that image to reflect a positive-type person, one who is alert but not tense and one who can meet challenges. You've got to look confident that you can convince your supervisor you're more than worth every dollar the company pays you.

For this reason, your physical appearance as a negotiator is of utmost importance. How you dress will reflect your personality, credibility, and appropriate management position. A dark suit or dress conveys authority, but black should be avoided as too negative. Long-sleeved shirts or blouses are more appropriate than short-sleeved ones. Shoes should be styled conservatively (no sneakers!), free from scuffs, and color-coordinated with the rest of the outfit. For men, a narrow-striped or a conservative print tie is proper; socks should be dark and should not sag around the ankles. Women should avoid saucer-size earrings and other ornate jewelry, mid-thigh skirts, and makeup so heavy that it distracts the listener from what they have to say. If your supervisor works without a jacket and with sleeves rolled up, you too can lighten up a little. Here's a common sense rule: To negotiate a raise, dress slightly more, not less, conservatively than your supervisor.

Eye contact connotes friendship, trust, and self-confidence, but staring may indicate hostility and disrespect. A warm smile is fine, but it should be sincere, not a mechanical display of teeth. Since dry lips show fear and tension, keep your lips moist. Coughing often projects nervousness unless, of course, you obviously have a cold. Have a clean handkerchief handy to cover unexpected sneezes.

2. Speech Is Important Too

A well-modulated tone—but not monotone—and crisp pronunciation of words, without slurring, will help in projecting a good impression. Clear diction and a proper command of language, including use of an adequate vocabulary and proper grammar, are essential. However, don't attempt to impress your supervisor by using six-syllable words when simple language will put your message across. And remember: never raise your voice, especially if you are angry.

3. Watching for Body Language

Body language may be used to project a person's true personality or to convey false signals. The primary component of body language is eye contact. Prolonged scrutiny can make you feel ill at ease. If, on the other hand, a listener continually glances in other directions while you are talking, he or she is either disturbed by what you are saying or is not paying full attention. Continual blinking can indicate anger, excitement, or fear. Eyebrow twitching reflects nervousness.

Facial gestures and head movements can also project feelings or thoughts. Cocking the head may indicate interest or doubt. A warm smile usually denotes friendliness and agreement; a frown, sadness or anger.

Other types of body language include hand signals (clenched or opened fists) and arm and leg movements. A firm handshake indicates confidence; the "bone-crusher" may show insecurity; and the wet and clammy handshake reflects nervousness. Clenched fists often show anger and hostility. A tapping foot betrays impatience.

In *Winning by Negotiation,* Dr. Tessa Warschaw emphasizes that you must "pay attention to how you move" and watch your "signals and styles." "Signals are like magnets," she says, "putting out positive and negative energy that either attracts or repels other people." Intimidation signals force others to listen, or control when and when not these others may speak: ". . . raise your eyebrows or throw hard glances to express disapproval, turn your body away if you don't like what is being said, rise, read a memo on your desk or start to make a phone call when you want to end the meeting." A desire for solitude is shown by silence; "involuntary signals include facial and body twitches, jiggling legs and knees, nervous hands." Signs of approval include nodding one's head, flashing friendly glances, and the like. "But if your intent is to create a dialogue," Dr. Warschaw emphasizes, "your expressions will convey concern and care and genuine interest, and you'll give the other person the time needed to respond."

As you will have surmised by now, body language is a course in itself; it involves studying details of movement that are much more intricate than those described here. Much of what we know about this fascinating subject is learned by experience.

4. "How Did I Do?"

Self-assessment will help you to gain insight into your personality traits and your skills as a negotiator. By employing a checklist, it is possible to determine how well the negotiation was conducted and, in particular, how you appeared to your supervisor.

During the session, did you:

- follow your plan as you had prepared it?
- let your supervisor finish speaking without interrupting?
- avoid being offensive or argumentive? (This is where the "Yes, but . . ." technique may have come in handy.)
- answer questions directly without deviating from your salary objectives?
- avoid making concessions out of fear?
- pay careful attention to your own body language:
- avoid distracting mannerisms such as tapping your fingers or a pencil, wringing your hands, fidgeting, and touching your face?
- avoid obvious reactions to tension such as yawning, twitching, and perspiring?
- speak firmly and lucidly in a crisp, friendly, and audible tone?
- control the manner of presentation so that you appeared cordial and self-confident but not arrogant?
- observe the signals that indicated:

1. how friendly your supervisor felt upon greeting you? 2. when you should stop your presentation?

ANALYZING THE NEGOTIATION

CHAPTER 9

CASE STUDIES:

*Do's and Don'ts
in Negotiating
for a Raise*

If you strive for the best, why settle for the worst?

—Rabbi Stephen S. Wise

L et's consider three common situations that may be encountered in salary administration: getting an acceptable salary increase, getting a raise before it's due, and negotiating a raise that accompanies a promotion.

PRINCIPLE 9

There's a right way and a wrong way—but once you find the right way, stick with it!

In all of the cases illustrated below, the two parties are identified as follows:

E = Employee
S = Supervisor

CASE 1. GETTING AN ACCEPTABLE SALARY INCREASE

The Wrong Way

E: Say, Mr. S, can we get together? I'd like to discuss getting a raise.

S: Sure, why not? Come into my office now.

E: I haven't had a raise for a year. How about it? Aren't I past due?

S: It just so happens your raise is in the works, and you'll get it next month.

E: That's great! Now I have something to look forward to!

(*Critique:* So what went wrong? He got a raise! *But* he didn't bother finding out how much it was, nor was he prepared to negotiate to increase the amount if too low.)

The Negotiated Way

(The Preliminary)

E: Mr. S, at your convenience, I would like to discuss with you something of importance to both of us.

S: What is it?

E: I'd rather not discuss it out in the open since it's a private matter. If you could set up a time that is convenient to you, I'd appreciate it. It shouldn't take more than 15 minutes.

S: How about 3 o'clock this afternoon in my office?

E: Thank you, that would be fine.

(The meeting)

E: Mr. S, I haven't had an increase in salary in quite a while. Up to now, I was getting raises on an annual basis, but it has been more than a year since my last one. What's going on?

S: As you are aware, E, the company's profits have been down and the immediate future doesn't look too bright. As a result, the interval between raises has been extended.

E: As you know, I've been a loyal employee. But if the company is in such a predicament, perhaps it's risky to remain here. Don't misunderstand me, I want to stay with the company for many years to come, but I expect some recognition and remuneration in return.

S: You know I've been satisfied with you. In fact, I put you in for a raise, but it has been delayed along with the others. Let me see if I can get salary administration to expedite its approval. I'll get back to you as soon as I can.

E: Before we break off this meeting, can you give me an indication of how much of a raise I can expect and when it will be in my paycheck?

S: Sure, the increase is for $X, and it will be included in your paycheck one month from the time of approval.

E: But, Mr. S, that increase is less than the cost-of-living increase for the year. I know I won't be satisfied, nor, especially, will my wife, if it's not more.

S: Why, what amount did you have in mind?

E: (*E is prepared with an acceptable salary range and now cites the top figure. He also provides backup by referring to his activity log book, which shows outstanding job performance and other positive factors.*)

S: Wow, that's almost as much as I make!

E: Then it looks as though you're being underpaid, just like me.

S: I must admit that I wasn't aware of all the outstanding things you've done over the past year, and I certainly don't want to lose you. I'll tell you what I'll do: I'll try to bump your raise up to $Y. Is that satisfactory?

E: That's better, but it still falls $Z short of what I'd consider satisfactory. (*Even though $Y falls within the bottom of the acceptable salary range, E tries a higher counteroffer.*)

S: In that case, I think perhaps we may have to delay your raise until the next scheduled review. If you wait another few months, we may be able to get you a little more than $Y, but I can't guarantee it!

E: (*Thinking to himself: I had better quit while I'm ahead. A bird in the hand is worth two in the bush. Get that raise now, and plan for a better one in the future.*) Although I believe—and it looks as though you recognize—that I deserve a larger raise, in consideration of the company's dilemma I'll accept the $Y raise for now. Thank you in advance for any future efforts to provide more adequate increases! I certainly will be in there pitching to get the company over the hurdle. Please let me know when I can help and how.

S: Thank you for your consideration and cooperation. Keep up the good work, and together with the top-notch efforts of the other managers, we will help the company get over this tough time.

(*Critique:* In this example, the first offer is shown not to be the final one. Some employees believe a supervisor's offer is locked into one number, regardless of a company's financial position. Often, it is intimidating for an employee to make a counteroffer, especially if he or she likes the job and plans to stay for a long time. Nevertheless, there is always an opportunity to negotiate, particularly if done cooperatively without creating friction.)

CASE 2. GETTING A RAISE BEFORE IT'S DUE

The Wrong Way

E: Ms. S, this inflation is killing me: fuel prices keep rising, the cost of electricity is up, and the damn taxes just rose another 10 percent. I need a raise just to meet these increases.

S: I would like to give you a raise, but my departmental budget won't permit it. You've been here long enough to know that raises are given only on an annual basis.

E: I figured that would be your answer, but I decided to take a chance and ask you anyway!

(*Critique:* E was unprepared for the meeting (he should have been ready to argue his worth to the company) and gave up too soon.)

The Negotiated Way

E: In the six months since my last salary review, I have taken over the responsibilities of Mr. X as well as retaining my own duties. Since he left the department, you turned over his accounts to me. While this additional work is challenging and I enjoy it, I believe it warrants additional compensation.

S: I certainly appreciate your taking on a bigger workload and the satisfactory performance you continue to demonstrate. But there is no money available for raises at this time.

E: Nevertheless, as we are both aware, Ms. S, the company's revenues and profits are up sharply from last year. I feel that my work contributed to these increases and that a raise is justifiable for me at this time.

S: You've been here long enough to know that the company's policy is to award raises only once a year, and we're only halfway through that period.

E: But we both know that policies can be bent. Suppose someone decides to leave? Wouldn't management provide an interim raise to keep a good worker? Don't get me wrong. I don't want to leave. I like it here and enjoy my work.

S: Well, we could make an exception for a special case, but yours is not unusual.

E: Isn't it a special case if an employee is not being paid in accordance with what he is contributing? My workload has increased immensely, and I've taken on the additional responsibilities without griping. I know I'm doing an excellent job, and I'm sure the company and especially you want to continue to treat me fairly.

S: Others in our department are contributing more than what is expected of their positions, and they're satisfied; they aren't asking for raises.

E: (*At this point, the activity log is displayed and thumbed through.*) I'm sure that you can be proud of your department's output, but I cannot speak for others. The extra work I've undertaken imposes more responsibilities for additional skills and requires devoting spare time to study things more carefully. I've even given up my weekly golf game!

S: I guess I haven't fully realized the situation and its impact on your workload. Give me some time to talk it over with salary administration to see whether there's a chance of getting an interim raise for you. I'll get back to you within the week.

E: Thank you, Ms. S, I appreciate your consideration.

(The next meeting, a week later)

S: I'm pleased to inform you that you are being considered for a promotion and, of course, an accompanying raise within the normal review period. But in appreciation of your excellent performance, I have stressed to salary administration that you have earned a raise and they concurred to grant an interim increase of $X. I hope this is satisfactory.

E: I really am pleased, *especially* in looking forward to that promotion! Thank you, Ms. S!

(Critique: The supervisor was forced to reveal that a promotion was being considered. Gaining an interim raise on top of a coming promotion certainly was a coup. Also, the employee did not require an extensive effort to convince his boss of the outstanding performance. Probably the activity log helped to promote the interim raise.)

CASE 3. NEGOTIATING THE RAISE ACCOMPANYING A PROMOTION

The Wrong Way

S: I thought that getting the promotion you've been promised would please you. And the increase in salary is indeed commensurate with the new title. I can't understand why you're not satisfied. What salary would you be happy with?

E: I'm making $XX,XXX now and would have expected at least a 10 percent increase.

S: Well, a 6 percent increase is standard policy with any promotion in this company. You do want this promotion, don't you?

E: Sure I do! Oh, well, I guess I'd better be satisfied with the regular increase.

(Critique: E gave in too easily and did not show confidence in his own worth.)

The Negotiated Way

S: I thought getting the promotion you've been promised would please you. And the increase in salary is indeed commensurate with the new title. I can't understand why you're not satisfied. What salary would you be happy with?

E: I think you can understand better than anyone else, what raise should accompany a promotion—certainly not one that is just equal to a merit raise. I request that you reconsider what may be suitable.

S: I think you should consider the promotion and not be too concerned with salary. After all, the promotion does place you in another bracket and provides you with a broader salary range and chances for more raises!

E: Certainly you are right, but I don't want to wait another year until the next merit review before getting another raise. I would feel cheated by losing out on a whole year's difference in salary.

S: I hate to think how grumpy you may be until next year when salary review occurs again. Of course, you realize that you wouldn't have gotten this promotion unless I thought you had earned it. So let's hear what salary would satisfy you.

E: Before getting back to the salary, I'd like to know more about my new job responsibilities. Tell me more about how the departmental structure will change and who will report to me. Also, what are some of your plans for the growth of our department in the near and far future?

S: The main objective this coming year is to increase the number of subcontracts and purchase orders we process. For this reason, we are computerizing and automating the issuance of requests for quotations and purchase orders. Some of the people who are your peers in your current position will be reporting to you. You will be performing some of my duties, relieving me of those responsibilities and giving me time to plan the expansion and reorganization of the department. We anticipate that the company's revenues will increase steadily over the next five years. This growth may depend on the contributions of many departments, including ours, to make the company more competitive.

E: It all sounds great. But let me return to the subject at hand. In the new position, what is the salary range? And, will the frequency of salary reviews be the same as in my current position?

S: Your performance will be appraised and your salary reviewed annually. If you are performing as well as you are doing now, there's no reason not to expect annual increases. As for the range, it has been established by salary administration and falls between $$XX,XXX$ and $$XY,YYY$. But let me point out that, if you had an MBA, your starting salary for the new position could be on the higher, not the lower, end of the scale.

E: Apparently you're not convinced that I've been doing more than just a satisfactory job. Let's take a moment to review what I've accomplished since the last performance appraisal. (*E's activity log is presented and reviewed; her outstanding accomplishments are emphasized.*) According to my job performance, I think you might agree that the salary should be toward midrange. And if I'm taking on part of your job, don't you think the salary should be more in line with what those in your job classification are earning? Certainly my qualifications and accomplishments warrant a better increase than 6 percent.

S: But you don't have an advanced degree, and you must be trained for the new position. The company will provide you with training on company time; that's a major concession.

E: Well, I haven't brought you completely up to date on my background. As for the MBA, I expect to complete my studies and be awarded a degree next year. Also, in my spare time, I have been attending various workshops and seminars under the auspices of the NCMA that cover contractual matters. These courses should provide most of the knowledge necessary to perform the new job and, I think you would agree, should suffice in lieu of the on-the-job training that I would have received from the company.

S: Well, as I said, the company has established $$XX,XXX$ as the starting level for the new position, but let me advise salary administration of your additional qualifications, of which I must admit I was unaware. I'll get back to you later this week.

E: I know that I may have put you in a difficult position, and I do appreciate your efforts. I certainly can wait a week for your response. Thank you.

S: Okay, see you then.

(A phone call two days later)

S: Would it be satisfactory to you if we started you at $*XX,XXX* with the agreement that you will receive an increase at a level closer to your expectations after a six-month trial period?

E: That sounds fair enough. Let me think about it. Can you wait two days for my answer?

S: Yes, but I would expect that it will be affirmative.

(*Critique:* This case exemplifies a salary offer-and-counter-offer procedure. Note that E was aware of what constituted a more acceptable percentage for a raise accompanying a promotion. She had done her homework and was prepared to defend her worth. On the other hand, S did not prepare adequately since he was unaware of E's pursuit of education. After all, S had been approving company-sponsored tuition-reimbursement checks for E's graduate work for a number of years and should have found out just what E was doing. As E pointed out, the additional training received outside of working hours would be cost effective in that the company need not conduct a training program for the new job, and E's time could be spent more productively.)

CHAPTER 10

ANALYZING HOW YOU WON THAT BIG RAISE AND LOOKING AHEAD

We dare not look back to great yesterdays. We must look forward to great tomorrows.

—*Adlai E. Stevenson*

After completion of the raise negotiation, which we presume turned out satisfactorily, you should record what transpired by recalling the sequence of events and analyzing what you did right, what you may have done wrong, and what your strong and weak points were as a negotiator. By recording this session in your activity log book, you will immediately prepare yourself for the next salary review and for future sessions. Refer to Chapter 8 and review the question "How Did I Do?"

PRINCIPLE 10

You got that big raise—now go for a promotion and more raises.

Now ask yourself these additional questions in regard to the negotiation:

- Did I review my accomplishments, and show how effective I have been in job performance and profitability to the firm?
- Did I compare my supervisor's goals against my performance objectives to ensure agreement?
- Did I let my supervisor make the first offer for a salary

increase and then negotiate a higher figure, using the initial offer as a jumping-off point?
- How does the raise compare, over the current year and for the past five years, with:
  (1) cost-of-living adjustment figures,
  (2) production workers' increases,
  (3) unionized workers' increases,
  (4) increases granted to other managerial levels,
  (5) increases for others in the same position, both inside and outside the department, and
  (6) increases cited in surveys for my occupation and location?
- Were fringe benefits offered, and, if so, what did I accept?
- What are the dollar-value equivalents of the fringe benefits I accepted?

In Philip Sperber's book *Fail-Safe Business Negotiating,* five strategies for job advancement are identified that may be adapted and compared with the strategies and tactics you used in negotiating your raise. It may be helpful to keep Sperber's strategies in mind (and in your log book) for the next time:

1. You demonstrate that you take on responsibility and are promotable by impressing your supervisor to reach that conclusion.
2. You assist your supervisor by supportive, outstanding (or, at least, good) performance to make him or her look "good" to management.
3. You play to your supervisor's ego and emotional needs so as to enhance your chances for a promotion or a better raise.
4. Your performance excels to such a degree that your rating is top-notch in the job-appraisal rating system employed by the company.
5. You project a good image and make it visible to not only your supervisor but also your supervisor's superiors and any other member(s) of higher management that

you may encounter during the course of performing your job.

An article in *Fortune* magazine entitled "Is Your Career on Track?" states, "Gauging your career progress has always been more an art than science, but what on earth are you supposed to make of the signals you're getting now?" In the past, the "organization man" looked forward to a career that moved upward with promotions coming every two years, where personal feelings were secondary to corporate support, success equated to job security through retirement, "good pay" was age times $1,000, and a 40-hour workweek was standard. Today's manager expects lateral moves as routine (or even desirable), with responsibilities increasing with fewer title changes. Success may equate to salary level more than personal satisfaction, with compensation including bonuses and profit sharing. The manager will probably work until a particular assignment is completed, regardless of the time it may take.

"Promotions are slowing down for another reason," the article continues. "Many companies that once moved the best and the brightest on a fast track to a new job every 12 to 18 months are wondering if that isn't too fast." So what can you expect if your management is following that trend? More frequent and better raises instead of promotions? That, of course, is another consideration and should provide impetus in getting a bigger raise, now and in the future. In the past, salaries and promotions were almost synonymous, and "big" raises accompanied promotions. Today, the emphasis is on compensation in any form—dollars or other, comparable benefits.

Management currently expects more from managers in taking on responsibilities in situations where they may receive rewards later (i.e., end-of-the-year bonuses) for demonstrating excellence in performance. But companies may not recognize employee dissatisfaction if there is a lack of employee recognition in the form of promotions, as well as compensation. In times of prosperity, dissatisfaction is manifested by high employee turnover, or an unusual number of middle managers deciding to start their own businesses to satisfy their thirst for accomplishment and recognition. When the economy is recessional, however, companies can demand more from the employees at lower compensation levels. Of course, top management considers profit the number-one priority, even to the point of sacrificing top-notch managers and eliminating strategic-planning departments. This policy may well be short-sighted, since these employees may have been the "brains" of an organization and may have been responsible for reshaping the firm to improve profitability in future years. Today the world is in a hurry—company managers have lost patience and can't wait for higher profits to become visible. A year of lower profits may mean decreased stock prices and a reduction in the value of stock holdings by top management.

So where do you, as a manager, go from here? One sensible course is to improve your negotiation techniques, which not only assist in the attainment of better raises now but also will be valuable in future employment opportunities. As indicated earlier, negotiation techniques are something that everyone can learn to employ as an additional aid for achieving success. Also, the techniques may help to foster a positive mental attitude and provide know-how in responding to negative replies or in converting negative answers into positive ones. For example, if your supervisor said, "You were turned down for a raise because you lack certain experience or qualifications," you might reply, "If I could prove to you that I am qualified, would you give me the increase?" As an effective negotiator, you would be able to keep the dialogue going until a satisfactory response was received.

THE AUTHOR'S TEN PRINCIPLES FOR NEGOTIATING RAISES

1. *If a CEO's average raise is 30 percent per annum and a production worker's is 5 percent, certainly a manager's raise should be somewhere in between these extremes.*

2. *Know your adversary.*

3. *Job relevancy is important, but personal achievement is better.*

4. *Job evaluations and appraisals may measure managerial performance, but without adequate raises they are meaningless.*

5. *Plan your moves; then move your plans.*

6. *You probably won't get everything you ask for, but you can surely try!*

7. *To be considered successful, a salary negotiation should leave both parties feeling as though they have won something; you, a satisfactory raise; your supervisor, a contented, productive manager.*

8. *Stop: look at and listen to yourself, and visualize how others see you.*

9. *There's a right way or a wrong way—but once you find the right way, stick with it!*

10. *You got that big raise—now go for a promotion and more raises.*

REFERENCES: MORE ABOUT SALARIES AND RAISES

Aggarwal, Sumer C., and Sudhir, "A Management Rewards System for the Long and Short Terms," *Personnel Journal*, December 1986, pp. 115–121.

Aldrich, Mark, and Robert Buchele, *The Economics of Comparable Worth*, Ballinger Publishing Co., Cambridge, 1986.

Beier, Ernst G., and Evans G. Valens, *People-Reading*, Warner Books, New York, 1975.

Belcher, David W., *Compensation Administration*, Prentice-Hall, Englewood Cliffs, NJ, 1974.

Bennett, Amanda, "Caught in the Middle," *The Wall Street Journal*, April 18, 1990, pp. R9 and R10.

Berne, Eric, *Games People Play*, Grove Press, New York, 1964.

Chapman, Jack, *How to Make $1,000 a Minute: Negotiating Salaries and Raises*, Ten Speed Press, Berkeley, CA, 1987.

Chastain, Sherry, *Winning the Salary Game*, John Wiley & Sons, New York, 1980.

Crystal, Graef S., "Seeking the Sense in CEO Pay," *Fortune*, June 5, 1989, pp. 90–104.

——, "The Great CEO Pay Sweepstakes," *Fortune*, June 18, 1990, pp. 94–102.

"Eleventh Annual Salary Survey," *Working Woman*, January 1990, pp. 105–112.

Farnham, Alan, "The Trust Gap," *Fortune*, December 4, 1989, pp. 56–78.

Fierman, Jaclyn, "The People Who Set the CEO's Pay," *Fortune*, March 12, 1990, pp. 58–66.

Hegarty, Christopher, and Philip Goldberg, *How to Manage Your Boss*, Rawson, Wade Publishers, New York, 1980.

Jensen, Michael C., and Kevin J. Murphy, "CEO Incentives—It's Not How Much You Pay, But How," *Harvard Business Review*, May–June 1990, pp. 138–154.

Karrass, Chester L., *Give and Take*, Thomas Y. Crowell, New York, 1974.

Kennedy, Joyce Lance, *Higher Salaries: How to Get Them,* Sun Features, Cardiff, CA, 1983.

Kennedy, Marilyn Moats, *Salary Strategies,* Rawson, Wade Publishers, New York, 1982.

Kirkpatrick, David, "Is Your Career on Track?" *Fortune,* July 2, 1990, pp. 38–48.

Kravetz, Dennis J., *Getting Noticed,* John Wiley & Sons, New York, 1985.

Meredith, David R., "Its Not How Much, But How," *Chief Executive,* September–October 1989, pp. 24–34.

Nierenberg, G., and H. Calero, *How to Read a Person Like a Book,* Pocket Books, New York, 1971.

Paterson, T. T., *Job Evaluation,* Volume 2, Business Books, London, 1978.

Pease, Allan, *Signals: How to Use Body Language for Power, Success and Love,* Bantam Books, New York, 1981.

Schatzki, M., and W. R. Coffey, *Negotiation: The Art of Getting What You Want,* Signet Books, New York, 1981.

Sherer, Peter D., Donald P. Schwab, and Herbert G. Heneman, "Managerial Salary-Raise Decisions," *Personnel Psychology,* Spring 1987, pp. 27–39.

Silber, Mark B., and V. Clayton Sherman, *Managerial Performance and Promotability,* AMACOM, New York, 1974.

Sperber, Philip, *Fail-Safe Business Negotiating,* Prentice-Hall, Englewood Cliffs, NJ, 1983.

Tarkenton, Fran, *Playing to Win,* Harper & Row, New York, 1984.

Thakur, Manab N., Paul DuMont, and Herff Moore, "Achieving Managerial Pay Equity," *Compensation and Benefits Review,* July–August 1988, pp. 29–40.

Warschaw, Tessa A., *Winning by Negotiation,* McGraw-Hill, New York, 1980.

Wenzel, Tina G., "Because I'm Worth It," *The Secretary,* June–July 1990, pp. 14 and 15.

INDEX

The
Cassell
Business Success Guides
Series

Writing Effective Letters and Memos
0 304 34461 3

Winning with Difficult People
0 304 34460 5

Delegating Authority
0 304 34459 1

How to Negotiate a Bigger Raise
0 304 34458 3